THE VALUE OF IMAGINATION

The Story of Charles Dickens

VALUE COMMUNICATIONS, INC.
PUBLISHERS
LA JOLLA, CALIFORNIA

THE VALUE OF IMAGINATION

The Story of
Charles Dickens

BY SPENCER JOHNSON, M.D.

First Edition
Manufactured in the United States of America
For further information write to: ValueTales, P.O. Box 1012
La Jolla, CA 92038

Library of Congress Cataloging in Publication Data

Johnson, Spencer.
    The value of imagination.

    (ValueTales)
    SUMMARY: A biography of the nineteenth-century
English novelist, Charles Dickens, emphasizing the value of
an imaginative mind.
    1.   Dickens, Charles, 1812–1870—Biography—Juvenile
literature.   2.   Novelists, English—19th century—
Biography—Juvenile literature.   3.   Imagination—Juvenile
literature.   [1.   Dickens, Charles, 1812–1870.   2.   Authors,
English.   3.   Imagination.]   I.   Pileggi, Steve.   II.   Title.
PR4581.J66   823'.8 [B] [92]   77-13947

ISBN 0-916392-15-5

Dedicated to Steve Pileggi
whose imagination is fun to see.

This tale is about the imaginative Charles
Dickens. The story that follows is based on
events in his life. More historical facts about
Charles Dickens can be found on page 63.

Once upon a time...

long, long ago, there lived in England a little boy named Charles Dickens.

Charles was a happy lad. He especially loved the stories his father told. In the evenings, his brothers and sisters sat listening to their father and sipping the hot lemon punch their mother made for them. Charles sat listening and dreaming grand dreams.

"When I grow up," Charles thought, "I'm going to be a great storyteller too—just like my dad!"

Sometimes, when Mr. Dickens wasn't telling marvelous stories, he took young Charles for long, rambling walks. Once, when he and Charles were out together, they came to a place called Gad's Hill, and they stopped to admire a grand mansion there.

"Daddy," said Charles, "some day I'm going to live in that house." Then Charles closed his eyes, and he told his father exactly how grand it was going to be when he lived there.

Mr. Dickens laughed. "You have a great imagination, Charles," he said.

"Imagination? What does that mean?" asked Charles.

"Well," said Mr. Dickens, "it means being able to take something real—like that house—and use it to make pictures in your mind of something that isn't real yet—like the way you think it will be when you live in that house."

"I see," said Charles. "It's fun to use imagination!"

"Of course it is," said his father. And they walked home.

9

The little house where Charles lived with his family was not elegant like the mansion at Gad's Hill. Just the same, Charles liked his home very much.

He also liked going over to the house next door, where Mr. Giles lived. Mr. Giles had piles and heaps of books, and he was teaching Charles to read.

"But haven't you any books of your own?" Mr. Giles asked Charles one day.

"Well, sir, I did once see some old books in our attic," said Charles, "but I never looked inside them."

"Then for goodness sake, hurry home and look into them!" cried Mr. Giles. "See what's waiting for you in your own attic."

Charles ran off as fast as he could, thinking, "I wonder what I will find?"

He trotted into his own house and climbed up the stairs. He threw open the attic door, and there were the books.

"I wonder how they got here," said Charles to himself. "They look so old and dusty. But maybe if I clean them off, I'll find some good ones."

"My dear little chap," said a strange, small voice, "of course you'll find some good ones!"

Charles jumped, and he almost cried out with fright.

"I beg your pardon, young man," said the little creature who had come out from behind a row of books. "I didn't mean to startle you!"

"Wh . . . who are you?" asked Charles.

"My name is B.W.," said the little creature. "That's short for Bookworm."

"And what," Charles asked, "is a bookworm?"

The little creature explained that a bookworm is a worm that lives in books and eats their pages.

"I see," said Charles politely. "But I never knew that a worm could talk. Are you real, B.W., or did I make you up? Sometimes I *do* make things up."

"I thought so," said the bookworm, and he laughed.

Charles knew then that he had imagined the bookworm, just as he had imagined living someday in the big house on Gad's Hill. But it was fun to imagine, and Charles decided that he wouldn't stop. "Tell me more about yourself," he said to B.W.

"I'm a very special bookworm," said B.W. "I never eat the printed part of a page. I only nibble on the white part at the edges. That way I can always go back and read what's in the book. And that way I meet some very interesting characters."

"Characters?" asked Charles. "What are characters?"

"Characters, my curious young friend, are the people who live in books," said B.W. "Some of them are quite enchanting. Look around and you'll see!"

Young Charles looked around the attic, and suddenly it was crowded with people who seemed to appear out of the books that were piled on the shelves.

"That's Robinson Crusoe!" cried B.W. "I know him. And there's Don Quixote! And see those shieks over there? They're from the *Arabian Nights*!" B.W. knew them all because he had read all the books in the attic.

"What fun!" cried Charles.

"Books *are* fun!" Charles decided. "And using my *own* imagination to pretend about things is fun, too!"

"True," said B.W., "but let me warn you, young sir, that life demands more of you than imagination. Simply sitting on a curb and dreaming about great houses is a sure way to get nowhere. But when you do some real work, it is much more likely that your dreams will come true."

Charles went downstairs, with little B.W. tagging along, and he began to help his mother.

"See, it's not so bad," said B.W. "In fact, work really is a kind of fun, too."

But as much as the Dickens children helped out around the house, it wasn't enough. Something terrible was happening to the Dickens family.

What do you think it was?

The Dickens family was running out of money. Charles didn't understand why, but Mr. Dickens had long since lost his job. For a while Mr. Dickens had been able to borrow enough money to keep the family going. But now there wasn't even enough money for food. Things were very bad indeed.

Charles was worried. At that time, in England, people who were in debt—people who couldn't pay back the money they borrowed—could be arrested and sent to debtor's prison.

And finally, one bleak and unhappy day, there was a knock at the door. "Open up!" cried a voice from outside. "It's the police!"

"Mr. John Dickens sir," said one of the policemen to Charles' father, "can you pay back the money you owe to the shopkeepers?"

"I'm afraid I don't have enough money right now," answered Mr. Dickens.

"Then, sir, if you can't pay your bills, we must take you to debtor's prison," said the policeman sadly.

The children cried and wept, but the policemen had to take John Dickens off to the dreaded Marshalsea Prison.

Because they had no one to support them, Mrs. Dickens and the children had to move into the prison with Mr. Dickens. Young Charles was the only one who did not go to Marshalsea Prison. By this time he was old enough to work and he had gotten a job in a nearby factory.

Every day, after he finished his work, Charles went to visit his family in prison. And every day he thought, "How terrible! It's dirty here, and it smells bad. And how can any of these people ever pay their bills? When they're in prison, they can't work and make any money!"

22

"Charles," said his father, "when you look at me here, I hope you will think of ways to manage your own money more wisely, so that you never have to be in this place."

"I will," said Charles. "I'm sorry, but I must go now to my job. I love you." Charles waved a sad goodbye to his family, and headed out into the dark night.

23

Charles certainly thought of his family as he walked each night from the Marshalsea Prison to the old building where he lived in a little attic room at the top of the stairs. "How my happy life has changed," he thought as he went through the dark streets. "Whatever will become of me?"

He climbed the dingy, dusty stairs, promising himself that his life would be better. Whatever happened, he would take good care never to be in debtor's prison.

But he was terribly lonely there in his attic. He had only his little imaginary friend, B.W., to keep him company. And he had only bread and cheese to eat for his supper. Again and again, he thought, "What will I do? What will become of me?"

He worried as he went to sleep at night. And he felt sad as he woke in the gray dawn to go to work. Just the thought of the place where he worked made Charles feel ashamed.

What sort of place do you think it was?

25

It was a dark, dreary building near the river where they made black shoe polish. It was called a blacking factory. The floors were rotten and slimy, and the cold air was filled with foul smells. Rats scuttled over his feet as Charles tried to work. He and six other children sealed and labeled the bottles of shoe polish.

Charles was paid only a shilling a day for his work. And he had to pay almost that much for his room. He was often hungry, and he always seemed to be tired. Sometimes he tried to comfort himself by talking with his little make-believe friend, B.W.

B.W. tried to be cheerful, of course, but he didn't like the blacking factory, either. "Not the place for a gentle, sensitive soul like me," B.W. would say. "Oh, how I wish I were back with my books."

"I wish we were both back with our books," said Charles. "But even if I can't read right now, I can at least keep my mind busy. I'll play a little game. I'll notice everything that goes on here, and I'll remember it all."

And that is exactly what Charles did.

One day, Charles was taken ill at work, and he had to be sent home. One of the boys who worked with Charles was an orphan named Bob Fagin. "I'll go with you," said Bob. "I'll make sure you get safely to your door."

Now Charles was ashamed of the gloomy old building where he lived. And he didn't want his friend to see his shabby room at the top of the stairs. So when his friend kindly insisted on walking Charles right to his door, Charles played a little trick on him. What do you think Charles did?

He walked boldly up to the front door of a beautiful house, and he rang the doorbell. "Thanks for walking me home," he said to Bob Fagin. "I'll be fine now, and you can go back to work."

Bob Fagin left just before a butler answered the door. "What do *you* want?" said the butler to the poorly dressed boy on the doorstep.

"Is this the home of Mr. Robert Fagin?" asked Charles.

"Certainly not," said the butler. He slammed the door in Charles' face. Then Charles Dickens turned and very slowly walked home to his own little attic room.

While Charles was working in the blacking factory, his father was using his time in debtor's prison as wisely as he could. "I don't know how I'll ever get out of here," thought Mr. Dickens, "but when I do, I'll really have to support my family. And I know how I'll do it. I'll learn shorthand and get a job as a reporter."

So John Dickens got a book on shorthand. He read it over and over and he practiced again and again until he could write down whatever people said just as fast as they said it.

John Dickens soon had a chance to use his shorthand. A relative gave him enough money so that he could pay all his debts and be released from prison.

"That was a terrible experience," said Mr. Dickens.

As he had planned, he got a job as a reporter, recording things that happened in court. Then he hurried to find Charles and tell him the good news.

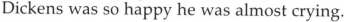

"Charles, my boy," he said, "you'll never have to work in a blacking factory again. From now on, I'll take care of you." Mr. Dickens was so happy he was almost crying.

"Great!" whispered B.W. to Charles. "You proved you can take care of yourself if you have to, but it will be a relief to get away from that dreadful factory."

"Can I go to school?" Charles asked his father.

"Yes. I'll even be able to send you to school," said Mr. Dickens.

Charles knew then that his father loved him very much, for in those days schools weren't free to everyone. In fact, they were very costly. And most people never even learned to read and write. Charles walked along, hand in hand with his father. He felt that a great, new, wonderful world awaited him.

33

Charles often enjoyed his school, and certainly B.W. felt right at home. "You're a clever little lad to study so hard," said B.W. "Reading is the greatest fun, and writing is terribly important."

"I know it's important," said Charles, "and I'm going to learn so much that I'll never have to work in a blacking factory again."

But Charles wasn't always studying. Sometimes he found time to get into mischief.

What do you think he did?

Once he and the other boys saw mice scurrying on the floor of a classroom, and they decided to hold mice races. The boys made toy chariots and then harnessed the mice to the chariots. The mice then raced for all they were worth, pulling the chariots across the room.

"Come on! Hurry up!" the boys shouted to their favorite racing mouse.

But then all of a sudden they heard a louder voice. "What's going on here?" an angry teacher demanded.

The boys, of course, were punished for playing with the mice.

"Very amusing," whispered B.W. "But don't you think you could find a better way to use your imagination?"

Charles still liked to pretend that the little bookworm talked with him. Of course, when he was listening to B.W., Charles was really listening to his own thoughts. He knew that very often the answers to your problems have to come from inside you.

"You can always learn by looking about you, Charles," B.W. seemed to say. "Study the people you see. Try to guess what they are thinking. Imagine what they are really like."

Charles began to watch people, and to really take notice of what they did and why they did it. He studied his friends and the stern headmaster. He saw the hard-working teacher and the kindly porter. He noticed places, too, and how they looked and smelled and felt.

Charles couldn't know it then, but the day would come when he would make good use of everything he had seen, learned, and remembered.

After he left school, Charles knew that he needed to get a job.

"Do you remember what your father did when *he* had to find a way to earn a living?" asked B.W.

"Yes," said Charles. "He studied shorthand and became a reporter," said Charles. "Say, I think I'll do the same thing! It will take a lot of practice, and I'll have to listen carefully and write down exactly what people say. But then I'll make a good living."

So Charles studied and he practiced.

When he felt that he was ready, Charles went to a newspaper called *The True Sun* and asked for a job. "I can write shorthand," he told the editor. "I've studied well and I'm not afraid of work. I can do a good job for you."

Charles got the job! And he worked so well that before long he was given a most important assignment.

Charles' new assignment was to report what went on in the House of Parliament, the place where all of England's laws were made. In those days, there were about ninety reporters in Parliament. They each wrote the lawmakers' speeches down word for word in shorthand. Then they rewrote the speeches into longhand and rushed them to the newspapers, so that they could be published.

"Very impressive," said B.W. to Charles. "I'm quite proud of you. You're the youngest reporter ever to work in the House of Parliament!"

"I know, and it's fascinating work," said Charles. "But I don't see why so many laws are passed to help people in faraway lands while almost nothing is done to help the poor people right here in England."

But Charles didn't have much time to wonder about this. He had to pay very close attention to the speakers. And he had to be quick to get his reports to his newspaper before the other reporters got theirs to their newspapers. When he finished a report, he would dash out of Parliament and jump into a carriage—which in those days was the quickest way to get anywhere.

41

"Let's go!" he would shout to the coachman, and off they would race to the offices of *The True Sun*.

Charles reported the speeches so quickly and so well that his newspaper gave him extra money for doing such a good job.

Not that things always went well for him. Sometimes they didn't. In fact, once a wheel came off Charles' coach. The coach turned over and Charles and B.W. tumbled out onto the road.

Charles wasn't discouraged, though. And neither was B.W. A reporter has to expect a little upset now and then.

"Well, I suppose we can't always be first," laughed B.W.

One day Charles got tired of writing down only what other people said. He decided to use his imagination and make up a story of his *own*.

"A first-rate idea!" said B.W. "Only make sure to make up stories about things that you really know something about."

Charles nodded. "I'll use only what I've noticed myself in all of my stories."

Then Charles went out to look at the city of London.

43

"Wow," exclaimed Charles Dickens. "There is so much to see."

Of course, Charles had been observing people since he had been a small child. Now, wherever he went, he saw how people looked and he noticed what they did and he listened to the way they spoke.

"It's exciting," he said. "I can hardly wait to get home and start on my stories."

When Charles did start writing, he worked easily and quickly. Whole crowds of characters were already there in his mind, just waiting for him to put them on paper. And each one of them was at least a bit like someone Charles had known.

"Now what will you do with your story?" B.W. asked when Charles had finished.

That night B.W. watched Charles quietly walk through London's dark streets to a place called Johnson's Court. *The Monthly Magazine* had its office there, and when Charles was sure no one was looking, he dropped his story into the letter box on the office door.

"By Jove! You act as if writing your *own* story is some sort of crime!" cried B.W. "You didn't even put your own name on the story. You said it was by someone called 'Boz'!"

"Because I'm afraid people may not like it," said the shy young man. "And I don't want to be embarrassed."

A month later, when the magazine came out, Charles wasn't at all embarrassed. "They printed it!" he shouted. "They printed my story! I'm an author!"

"Quite true," said B.W. "And a very good story it is. I shouldn't be surprised to learn that the magazine wanted more such tales by 'Boz.'"

Indeed, the magazine did want more of Charles' stories. The readers had really enjoyed the first one.

Charles Dickens was soon writing stories as fast as he could put pen to paper. "There are so many books in my head," he said to B.W. "I want to tell my stories just as quickly as I can."

"You never were one to dillydally," smiled B.W. "What will your books be about?"

"About things that I know because they've happened to me," said Charles. "About children working in factories. About families living in debtor's prison. About poor people being hungry. I'll make the stories fun to read, but perhaps after people have read them they'll do something about the things that are wrong with the world today."

"Right now, I am thinking about a man I made up called Mr. Pickwick. And I want to write about a stingy old man whom I have named Scrooge and a poor little boy whom I have named Tiny Tim. I'm going to call the story *A Christmas Carol*."

Charles Dickens did write his books about Mr. Pickwick, Scrooge, Tiny Tim, and about many other characters besides. In time, his books filled whole shelves.

"Not that any of them ever seem to stay on a shelf," said B.W., and he said it most proudly. "People are always taking them down and reading them. There doesn't seem to be any end to the books, and to the marvelous characters who live in your books!"

And what sort of people do you think read Charles Dickens' books?

They were all types of people—princes and parlormaids, lords and ladies, servants and coachmen, young and old. One and all, they were fascinated by the men and women and children who were brought to life by Charles Dickens' imagination.

When they read a story by Dickens, people could picture the way it looked in a blacking factory. They could know more now how it felt to be in debtor's prison. The books caused people to use their own imaginations.

"People want your books," said B.W. to Charles, "but they want something else from you, too."

Can you guess what it was?

"They want to meet you, Charles," said the bookworm. "They want to hear you read your books out loud to them."

So Charles began to travel throughout England, reading to large audiences. People cried when he read to them about families in debtor's prison, or about children working long hours in dirty factories. And they laughed when he described parties and dances and wonderful trips into the country.

TONIGHT
Special Reading
BY
CHARLES
DICKENS

Charles Dickens' books were also very popular in America. Some people even went down to the wharfs to wait for the ships that came from England bringing the latest stories by Dickens. And when Dickens himself went to the United States to read his stories to people, there were enormous crowds at the pier to greet him.

While Charles was in America, something was happening in England.

What do you suppose it was?

Parliament was passing laws to protect children from having to work too hard and at too young an age. They were also passing laws closing the debtor's prisons and laws that made it possible for even poor children to go to school.

Many things were happening in England, including the fact that thousands of people had read Charles Dickens' stories. The stories made people think about how hard it was to be poor in England. And they wanted to make things better for everyone.

Then one night, after Charles returned from his trip to America, hundreds of people got together to tell him exactly what his books meant to them.

They gave a great dinner in Charles Dickens' honor in a gigantic dining room.

"Your imagination, Mr. Dickens, has given us great pleasure," said one of the hosts. "You have allowed us to meet some of the most interesting characters and to go inside some of the most unusual places simply by reading your books. You have become the most popular novelist of our times because your imagination has made our own lives more enjoyable. And you have helped to change some of our English laws, so that they are more fair to more people."

58

B.W. fought back a tear, and he sniffled—a thing that bookworms seldom do. And Charles Dickens felt proud and happy. Both of his childhood dreams had come true.

Do you remember what those two dreams were?

Charles Dickens dreamed about and worked very hard to become a great storyteller, and, indeed, he became one of the best in the land.

And, as you may remember, he also dreamed that one day he would live in the great house on Gad's Hill. And after he had written many books, he bought and lived in that very same house.

"I'm glad some of your dreams came true," B.W. said to Charles.

"Yes," said Charles, "but of course sometimes our dreams don't come true. What's more important is to have dreams. Just using my imagination makes me feel happy."

60

Perhaps you may want to think about how you feel when you use your imagination. What you choose to do with your imagination may be very different from what Charles Dickens did with his. But whatever you decide to do with your imagination, let's hope it makes you happier.

Just like it did for our good friend Charles Dickens.

The End

Charles John Huffam Dickens was born on February 7, 1812, the second of eight children. His early years were spent on the coast of southern England where his father, John Dickens, was a clerk in the Navy Pay Office in Portsmouth.

After losing his job, John Dickens moved his family to London, but continued to fare poorly. Eventually, a creditor forced John Dickens and most of his family into debtor's prison, where they spent three months.

During the time his family was in prison, Charles, who had just turned twelve, worked in a blacking factory on Old Hungerford Stairs. He found this experience so humiliating that he would seldom speak about it, even in his later life.

When his father was released from prison, Charles went to school at the Wellington House Academy, where the harsh proprietor and headmaster, a Welshman named Mr. Jones, punctuated the lessons with resounding blows on the pupils' backs with a swordlike cane. Nonetheless, Charles enjoyed the time he spent with books.

After he left school, Charles worked for a time as a London court reporter. And, at the age of twenty-one, he submitted his first story for publication. Under the pen name "Boz," a collection of these stories, which had become so popular, later appeared as a two-volume book—Dickens' first—entitled *Sketches By Boz*. Charles Dickens was then twenty-four years old.

In the meantime, young Charles continued to write. His next book, *Pickwick Papers*, was written and published, like most of his work, in installments. The first "chapter" sold only 400 copies, but by the time the fifteenth installment was ready, there were 40,000 advance orders. Charles Dickens, while still in his early twenties, was well on his way to becoming the most popular novelist of his time.

Dickens was primarily an entertaining storyteller, but he was also a social reformer. In 1850, he became the editor of a newspaper called *The Daily News*, which was established for the purposes of "combating evil, and advancing the welfare of the poor and the happiness of society." However, Dickens was considerably more effective as a storyteller. His entertaining books often opened the public's eyes to the faults of institutions. For the first time, more fortunate people were "allowed inside such places"

CHARLES DICKENS
1812–1870

through Dickens' characters and their own imaginations.

His books, including *Oliver Twist*, *Nicholas Nickleby*, *David Copperfield*, and *Little Dorritt*, helped crystallize English public opinion against abusive practices and institutions as debtor's laws, the school system, public almshouses, and child labor.

Dickens was nearly as well-known in the United States as he was in England, and he visited America twice. On his first visit, when he was thirty years old, Dickens was very disappointed in the ideal democracy he had imagined America was. His second visit, however, at the age of fifty-five, was considerably more enjoyable.

After a life of fame and recognition, Dickens died at the age of fifty-eight. He is buried with honor in the Poet's Corner of Westminster Abbey.

What pleased Dickens most, and what perhaps best illustrates the value of imagination, were comments like that of a woman who once approached him on the street in York. The woman, upon seeing him, exclaimed, "Mr. Dickens, let me touch the hand that has filled my home with many friends." And that of the old man in Belfast, Ireland, who, as he shook the hand of Charles Dickens, muttered, "God Bless You, Sir . . . for the light you've been in me house."

THE VALUE OF BELIEVING IN YOURSELF — The Story of Louis Pasteur

THE VALUE OF DETERMINATION — The Story of Helen Keller

THE VALUE OF PATIENCE — The Story of the Wright Brothers

THE VALUE OF KINDNESS — The Story of Elizabeth Fry

THE VALUE OF HUMOR — The Story of Will Rogers

THE VALUE OF TRUTH AND TRUST — The Story of Cochise

THE VALUE OF CARING — The Story of Eleanor Roosevelt

THE VALUE OF COURAGE — The Story of Jackie Robinson

THE VALUE OF CURIOSITY — The Story of Christopher Columbus

THE VALUE OF RESPECT — The Story of Abraham Lincoln

THE VALUE OF IMAGINATION — The Story of Charles Dickens

THE VALUE OF FAIRNESS — The Story of Nellie Bly

THE VALUE OF SAVING — The Story of Benjamin Franklin

THE VALUE OF LEARNING — The Story of Marie Curie

THE VALUE OF SHARING — The Story of the Mayo Brothers

THE VALUE OF RESPONSIBILITY — The Story of Ralph Bunche

THE VALUE OF HONESTY — The Story of Confucius

THE VALUE OF GIVING — The Story of Ludwig van Beethoven

THE VALUE OF UNDERSTANDING — The Story of Margaret Mead

THE VALUE OF LOVE — The Story of Johnny Appleseed

THE VALUE OF FORESIGHT — The Story of Thomas Jefferson

THE VALUE OF HELPING — The Story of Harriet Tubman

THE VALUE OF DEDICATION — The Story of Albert Schweitzer

THE VALUE OF FRIENDSHIP — The Story of Jane Addams

THE VALUE OF FANTASY — The Story of Hans Christian Andersen

THE VALUE OF ADVENTURE — The Story of Sacagawea

THE VALUE OF CREATIVITY — The Story of Thomas Edison